Country Poems

Country Poems

COMPILED BY

Caroline Foley

AURA

Images reproduced with permission from the following picture libraries:

AKG: 15, 20, 22, 36, 38, 51, 64, 69, 72

Art Archive/Picture Desk: 6, 11, 12, 16, 18, 24, 27, 28, 30, 32–33, 41, 47, 56, 60–61, 71, 75, 78, 82, 85, 86, 91, 95

Bridgeman Art Library: 54

Corbis: 8–9, 42, 58, 66, 76–77, 83, 92

Mary Evans: 34, 44, 48, 52, 63, 81, 88

This edition published in 2007
by Advanced Marketing (UK) Ltd,
Bicester, Oxfordshire

Copyright © 2006 Arcturus Publishing Limited
26/27 Bickels Yard, 151–153 Bermondsey Street,
London SE1 3HA

ISBN: 978-1-9057-6515-7

Editor: Belinda Jones
Art Director: Beatriz Waller
Cover design: Beatriz Waller
Design and layout: Laura Casella and Zoe Mellors

Printed in China

Contents

Introduction

The aim of this compilation of poetry, inspired by the countryside, was to provide a country basket of delights – pastoral verse plucked from the lofty heights of the Arcadian idyll of nymphs and shepherds down to the burlesque. However, as so much of the greatest poetry in the English language has been inspired by the countryside, the hardest choice was in deciding what to leave out.

In these pages you will find some of the most loved poems in the language. Marlowe's *The Passionate Shepherd to his Love* and Keats' *To Autumn* could not be left out. Along with Wordsworth's *Daffodils* is his *There Was a Boy*, the poem written about a lonely youth who summons owls with his wild hoots and halloos. Shakespeare is mainly represented by his songs. Both Tennyson, in *The Princess*, and Milton, in *Paradise Lost*, describe a summer night with such breathtaking poetic power that it was impossible not to include them.

One who gives a real flavour of countryside is Robert Herrick, a sixteenth-century rector who lends two extracts as seasonal openers for spring and autumn. His spirited country verses delivered from his pulpit had such impact on his parishioners that their descendents were able to recite them three hundred years later.

However, the sharply observed verses of John Clare, the eighteenth-century labourer's son who spent much of his life in Northampton General Asylum, have only recently come to be widely admired. Clare resisted all attempts from his publishers to change his words to the high-flown poetic language fashionable in his day: whilst others sing of cuckoos and nightingales, he describes the 'chimney sweeps' or crows in his *Sonnet: The Crow*.

Similarly, satirist Thomas Nashe, holed up in the country during the plague year of 1592, wrote a bird chorus in his *Summer's Last Will and Testament* so vivid that you can almost hear it, while Shakespeare mocked unfortunate cuckolds in the chorus of his song from *Love's Labour's Lost*, with his repetition of the cuckoo's cry.

A theme that runs through many of the poems is the parallel between the four seasons and man's own cycle of life. For this reason the most joyous poems, much concerned with love and romance, are inspired by the spring and summer. For elegance it would be difficult to better Thomas Carew, a favourite of Charles I, whose *The Spring* bemoans that his beloved carries 'June in her eyes, in her heart January'.

By autumn, a chill note enters with poems paying hommage to atmospheric, mist-laden scenes, whilst winter is a rightful mix of celebration and numb despair, brought about by the clear but frozen days at the end of the year. Happily, the anonymous sixteenth-century wintery song about a falconer losing and finding his hawk will bring a smile to most.

Finally, whilst most poems are kept in their recognized format and spelling, the poems on pages 13, 14, 17 and 21 have been reworked to improve the ease of read for a modern readership.

My hope is that amongst this miscellany of the joyous, the tragic and the comi-tragic, everyone will find a few verses that strike a chord or tug at a heartstring.

Caroline Foley 2005

I sing of brooks, of blossoms, birds, and bowers:
Of April, May, of June, and July-flowers.
I sing of May-poles, hock-carts, wassails, wakes,
Of bridegrooms, brides, and of their bridal cakes...

Spring

Sonnet: The Crow

John Clare

How peaceable it seems for lonely men
To see the crow fly in the thin blue sky
Over the woods and fields, o'er level fen.
It speaks of villages, or cottage nigh
Behind the neighbouring woods – when March winds high
Tear off the branches of the huge old oak.
I love to see these chimney-sweeps sail by
And hear them o'er the gnarled forest croak,
Then sosh askew from the hid woodman's stroke
That in the woods their daily labours ply.
I love the sooty crow, nor would provoke
Its March day exercise of croaking joy;
I love to see it sailing to and fro
While fields, and woods and waters spread below.

from The Prologue to

The Canterbury Tales

Geoffrey Chaucer

When that April with his showers sweet
Has pierced the drought of March to the root,
And bathed every vein in liquor of such power
By which virtue engendered is the flower,
When Zephyrus also with his sweet breath
Has quickened again in every grove and heath
Tender crops, and the young sun
Has in the Ram his half course run,
And small fowls make melody
That sleep away all the night with open eye
(So nature pricks them and their spirit urges)
Then people long to go on pilgrimages
And palmers go to seek strange strands
To distant shrines, known in sundry lands,
And specially, from every shire's end
Of England, down to Canterbury they wend
The holy blissful martyr for to seek,
That gave them help before when they were sick.

from
Love's Labour's Lost
William Shakespeare

When daisies pied and violets blue
And cuckoo-buds of yellow hue
And lady smocks all silver white
Do paint the meadows with delight,
The cuckoo then on every tree,
Mocks married men; for thus sings he;
Cuckoo.
Cuckoo, cuckoo! O word of fear,
Unpleasing to a married ear.

When shepherds pipe on oaten straws,
And merry larks are ploughman's clocks,
When turtles tread, and rooks and daws,
And maidens bleach their summer smocks,
The cuckoo then, on every tree,
Mocks married men, for thus sings he;
Cuckoo.
Cuckoo, cuckoo! O word of fear,
Unpleasing to a married ear.

from

The Passionate Shepherd to His Love

Christopher Marlowe

Come live with me, and be my love,
And we will all the pleasures prove,
That Vallies, groves, hills and fields,
Woods, or steepie mountain yields.

And we will sit upon the Rocks,
Seeing the Shepherds feed their flocks,
By shallow Rivers, to whose falls,
Melodious birds sing Madrigals.

And I will make thee beds of Roses,
And a thousand fragrant posies,
A cap of flowers, and a kirtle,
Embroidered all with leaves of Myrtle.

A gown made of the finest wool,
Which from our pretty Lambs we pull,
Fair linèd slippers for the cold:
With buckles of the purest gold.

A belt of straw, and Ivy buds,
With Coral clasps and Amber studs,
And if these pleasures may thee move,
Come live with me, and be my Love.

The Shepherds Swains shall dance and sing,
For they delight each May-morning.
If these delights thy mind may move;
Then live with me, and be my Love.

Spring

Gerard Manley Hopkins

Nothing is so beautiful as spring –
When weeds, in wheels, shoot long and lovely and lush;
Thrush's eggs look like little low heavens, and thrush
Through the echoing timber does so rinse and ring
The ear, it strikes like lightnings to hear him sing;
The glassy peartree leaves and blooms, they brush
The descending blue; that blue is all in a rush
With richness; the racing lambs too have fair their fling.

What is all this juice and all this joy?
A strain of the earth's sweet being in the beginning
In Eden garden. – Have, get, before it cloy,
Before it cloud, Christ, lord, and sour with sinning,
Innocent mind and Mayday in girl and boy,
Most, O maid's child, thy choice and worthy the winning.

from
Summer's Last Will and Testament

Thomas Nashe

Spring, the sweet spring, is the year's pleasant King,
When blooms each thing, then maids dance in a ring,
Cold doth not sting, the pretty birds do sing,
Cuckoo, jugge, jugge, pu we, to-witta-woo!

The Palm and May make country houses gay,
Lambs frisk and play, the Shepherds pipe all day,
And we hear aye birds tune this merry lay,
Cuckoo, jugge, jugge, pu we, to-witta-woo!

The fields breathe sweet, the daisies kiss our feet,
Young lovers meet, old wives a sunning sit;
In every street, these tunes our ears do greet,
Cuckoo, jugge, jugge, pu we, to-witta-woo!
Spring, the sweet spring.

The Spring

Thomas Carew

Now that winter's gone, the earth hath lost
Her snow-white robes, and now no more the frost
Candies the grass, or casts an icy cream
Upon the silver Lake, or Crystal stream:
But the warm Sun thaws the benumbèd Earth
And makes it tender, gives a sacred birth
To the dead Swallow; wakes in hollow tree
The drowsy Cuckoo, and the Humble-Bee.
Now do a choir of chirping Minstrels bring,
In triumph to the world, the youthful Spring.
The Valleys, hills, and woods, in rich array,
Welcome the coming of the long'd-for May,
Now all things smile; only my Love doth lour:
Nor hath the scalding Noon-day-Sun the power,
To melt that marble ice, which still doth hold
Her heart congeal'd, and makes her pity cold.
The Ox which lately did for shelter fly
Into the stall, doth now securely lie
In open fields; and love no more is made
By the fire side; but in the cooler shade
Amyntas now doth with his Cloris sleep
Under a Sycamore, and all things keep
Time with the season – only she doth carry
June in her eyes, in her heart January.

A Bird Came Down the Walk

Emily Dickinson

A Bird came down the Walk –
He did not know I saw –
He bit an Angleworm in halves
And ate the fellow, raw,

And then he drank the Dew
From a convenient Grass –
And then hopped sideways to the Wall
To let a Beetle pass –

He glanced with rapid eyes
That hurried all around –
They looked like frightened Beads, I thought –
He stirred his Velvet Head

Like one in danger, Cautious,
I offered him a Crumb
And he unrolled his feathers
And rowed him softer home –

Than Oars divide the Ocean,
Too silver for a seam –
Or butterflies, off Banks of Noon
Leap, plashless as they swim.

Daffodils

William Wordsworth

I wander'd lonely as a cloud
That floats on high o'er vales and hills,
When all at once I saw a crowd,
A host, of golden daffodils;
Beside the lake, beneath the trees,
Fluttering and dancing in the breeze.

Continuous as the stars that shine
And twinkle on the Milky Way,
They stretch'd in never-ending line
Along the margin of a bay:
Ten thousand saw I at a glance,
Tossing their heads in sprightly dance.

The waves besides them danced, but they
Out-did the sparkling waves in glee:
A poet could not but be gay,
In such a jocund company:
I gazed – and gazed – but little thought
What wealth the show to me had brought:

For oft, when on my couch I lie
In vacant or in pensive mood,
They flash upon that inward eye
Which is the bliss of solitude;
And then my heart with pleasure fills,
And dances with the daffodils.

Virtue

George Herbert

Sweet day, so cool, so calm, so bright,
The bridal of the earth and sky:
The dew shall weep thy fall to-night;
For thou must die.

Sweet rose, whose hue angry and brave
Bids the rash gazer wipe his eye:
The root is ever in its grave,
And thou must die.

Sweet spring, full of sweet days and roses,
A box where sweets compacted lie:
My music shows ye have your closes,
And all must die.

Only a sweet and virtuous soul,
Like seasoned timber, never gives;
But though the whole world turn to coal,
Then chiefly lives.

Home Thoughts from Abroad

Robert Browning

Oh, to be in England
Now that April's there,
And whoever wakes in England
Sees, some morning, unaware,
That the lowest boughs and the brushwood sheaf
Round the elm-tree bole are in tiny leaf,
While the chaffinch sings on the orchard bough
In England – now!

And after April, when May follows,
And the whitethroat builds, and all the swallows –
Hark! where my blossomed pear-tree in the hedge
Leans to the field and scatters on the clover
Blossoms and dewdrops – at the bent spray's edge –
That's the wise thrush; he sings each song twice over,
Lest you should think he never could recapture
That first fine careless rapture!
And though the fields look rough with hoary dew,
All will be gay when noontide wakes anew
The buttercups, the little children's dower
– Far brighter than this gaudy melon-flower!

…Summer days for me, When every leaf is on its tree;
When Robin's not a beggar, And Jenny Wren's a bride,
And larks hang singing, singing, singing,
Over the wheat-fields wide…

Summer

from
A Midsummer Night's Dream,
Act II Scene I
William Shakespeare

OBERON:
I know a bank whereon the wild thyme blows,
Where oxlips and the nodding violet grows
Quite over-canopied with luscious woodbine,
With sweet musk-roses, and with eglantine:
There sleeps Titania some time of the night,
Lull'd in these flowers with dances and delight;
And there the snake throws her enamell'd skin,
Weed wide enough to wrap a fairy in…

from

The Garden

Andrew Marvell

What wond'rous Life in this I lead!
Ripe Apples drop about my head;
The Luscious Clusters of the Vine
Upon my Mouth do crush their Wine;
The Nectaren, and curious Peach,
Into my hands themselves do reach;
Stumbling on Melons, as I pass,
Insnar'd with Flow'rs, I fall on Grass.

Mean while the Mind, from pleasure less,
Withdraws into its happiness:
The Mind, that Ocean where each kind
Does streight its own resemblance find;
Yet it creates, transcending these,
Far other Worlds, and other Seas;
Annihilating all that's made
To a green Thought in a green Shade.

Here at the Fountains sliding foot,
Or at some Fruit-trees mossy root,
Casting the Bodies Vest aside,
My Soul into the boughs does glide:
There like a Bird it sits, and sings,
Then whets, and combs its silver Wings;
And, till prepar'd for longer flight,
Waves in its Plumes the various Light.

Recipe for a Salad

Sydney Smith

To make this condiment, your poet begs
The pounded yellow of two hard-boiled eggs;
Two boiled potatoes, passed through kitchen-sieve,
Smoothness and softness to the salad give;
Let onion atoms lurk within the bowl,
And, half-suspected, animate the whole.
Of mordant mustard add a single spoon,
Distrust the condiment that bites so soon;
But deem it not, thou man of herbs, a fault,
To add a double quantity of salt.
And, lastly, o'er the flavoured compound toss
A magic soup-spoon of anchovy sauce.
Oh green and glorious! Oh, herbaceous treat!
'Twould tempt the dying anchorite to eat;
Back to the world he'd turn his fleeting soul,
And plunge his fingers in the salad bowl!
Serenely full, the epicure would say,
Fate can not harm me, I have dined today!

Heaven

Rupert Brooke

Fish (fly-replete, in depth of June,
Dawdling away their wat'ry noon)
Ponder deep wisdom, dark or clear,
Each secret fishy hope or fear.
Fish say, they have their Stream and Pond;
But is there anything Beyond?
This life cannot be All, they swear,
For how unpleasant, if it were!
One may not doubt that, somehow, Good
Shall come of Water and of Mud;
And, sure, the reverent eye must see
A Purpose in Liquidity.
We darkly know, by Faith we cry,
The future is not Wholly Dry.
Mud unto mud! – Death eddies near –
Not here the appointed End, not here!
But somewhere, beyond Space and Time,
Is wetter water, slimier slime!
And there (they trust) there swimmeth One
Who swam ere rivers were begun,
Immense, of fishy form and mind,
Squamous, omnipotent, and kind;
And under that Almighty Fin,
The littlest fish may enter in.
Oh! never fly conceals a hook,
Fish say, in the Eternal Brook,
But more than mundane weeds are there,
And mud, celestially fair;
Fat caterpillars drift around,
And Paradisal grubs are found;
Unfading moths, immortal flies,
And the worm that never dies.
And in that Heaven of all their wish,
There shall be no more land, say fish.

from

Paradise Lost

John Milton

Now came still Evening on, and Twilight grey
Had in her sober livery all things clad;
Silence accompanied; for beast and bird,
They to their grassy couch, these to their nests
Were slunk, all but the wakeful nightingale;
She all night long her amorous descant sung:
Silence was pleased. Now glowed the firmament
With living sapphires; Hesperus, that led
The starry host, rode brightest, till the Moon,
Rising in clouded majesty, at length
Apparent queen, unveiled her peerless light,
And o'er the dark her silver mantle threw.

from

Love in Secret

John Clare

I met her in the greenest dells,
Where dewdrops pearl the wood bluebells;
The lost breeze kissed her bright blue eye,
The bee kissed and went singing by,
A sunbeam found a passage there,
A gold chain round her neck so fair;
As secret as the wild bee's song
She lay there all the summer long.

I hid my love in field and town
Till e'en the breeze would knock me down;
The bees seemed singing ballads o'er,
The fly's bass turned a lion's roar;
And even silence found a tongue
To haunt me all the summer long;
The riddle nature could not prove
Was nothing else but secret love.

Standing Still

William Canton

Broad August burns in milky skies,
The world is blanched with hazy heat;
The vast green pasture, even, lies
Too hot and bright for eyes and feet.

Amid the grassy levels rears
The sycamore against the sun
The dark boughs of a hundred years
The emerald foliage of one.

Lulled in a dream of shade and sheen
With clement twilight thrown,
By that great cloud of floating green
A horse is standing, still as stone.

He stirs nor head nor hoof, although
The grass is fresh beneath the branch;
His tail alone swings to and fro
In graceful curves from haunch to haunch.

He stands quite lost, indifferent
To rock or pasture, trace or rein;
He feels the vaguely sweet content
Of perfect sloth in limb and brain.

Pied Beauty

Gerard Manley Hopkins

Glory be to God for dappled things –
For skies of couple-colour as a brinded cow;
For rose-moles all in stipple upon trout that swim;
Fresh-firecoal chestnut-falls; finches' wings;
Landscape plotted and pieced – fold, fallow and plough;
And all trades, their gear and tackle and trim.

All things counter, original, spare, strange;
Whatever is fickle, freckled (who knows how?)
With swift, slow; sweet, sour; adazzle, dim;
He fathers-forth whose beauty is past change:
Praise him.

Summer Night

from

'The Princess'

Alfred, Lord Tennyson

Now sleeps the crimson petal, now the white;
Nor waves the cypress in the palace walk;
Nor winks the gold fin in the porphyry font:
The fire-fly wakens: waken thou with me.

Now droops the milkwhite peacock like a ghost,
And like a ghost she glimmers on to me.

Now lies the Earth all Danaë to the stars,
And all thy heart lies open unto me.

Now slides the silent meteor on, and leaves
A shining furrow, as thy thoughts in me.

Now folds the lily all her sweetness up,
And slips into the bosom of the lake:
So fold thyself, my dearest, thou, and slip
Into my bosom and be lost in me.

from

There Was a Boy

William Wordsworth

There was a Boy; ye knew him well, ye cliffs
And islands of Winander! — many a time,
At evening, when the earliest stars began
To move along the edges of the hills,
Rising or setting, would he stand alone,
Beneath the trees, or by the glimmering lake;
And there, with fingers interwoven, both hands
Pressed closely palm to palm and to his mouth
Uplifted, he, as through an instrument,
Blew mimic hootings to the silent owls,
That they might answer him. — And they would shout
Across the watery vale, and shout again,
Responsive to his call, — with quivering peals,
And long halloos, and screams, and echoes loud
Redoubled and redoubled; concourse wild
Of jocund din! And, when there came a pause
Of silence such as baffled his best skill:
Then, sometimes, in that silence, while he hung
Listening, a gentle shock of mild surprise
Has carried far into his heart the voice
Of mountain-torrents; or the visible scene
Would enter unawares into his mind
With all its solemn imagery, its rocks,
Its woods, and that uncertain heaven received
Into the bosom of the steady lake.

I Saw in Louisiana a Live-Oak Growing

Walt Whitman

I saw in Louisiana a live-oak growing,
All alone stood it and the moss hung down from the branches,
Without any companion it grew there uttering joyous leaves
of dark green,
And its look, rude, unbending, lusty, made me think of myself,
But I wonder'd how it could utter joyous leaves standing alone there
without its friend near, for I knew I could not,
And I broke off a twig with a certain number of leaves upon it,
and twined around it a little moss,
And brought it away, and I have placed it in sight, in my room,
It is not needed to remind me as of my own dear friends,
(For I believe lately I think of little else than of them,)
Yet it remains to me a curious token, it makes me think of manly love;
And for all that, and though the live-oak glistens there
in Louisiana solitary in a wide flat space,
Uttering joyous leaves all its life without a friend or lover near,
I know very well I could not.

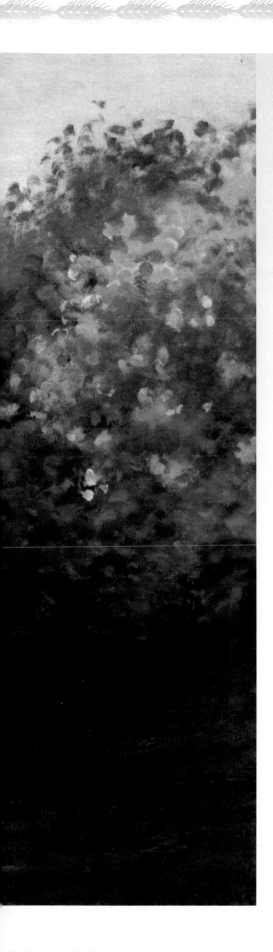

from
The Old Vicarage, Grantchester
Rupert Brooke

Just now the lilac is in bloom,
All before my little room;
And in my flower-beds, I think,
Smile the carnation and the pink;
And down the borders, well I know,
The poppy and the pansy blow…
Oh! There the chestnuts, summer through,
Beside the river make for you
A tunnel of green gloom, and sleep
Deeply above; and green and deep
The stream mysterious glides beneath,
Green as a dream and deep as death.
– Oh, damn! I know it! And I know
How the May fields all golden show,
And when the day is young and sweet,
Gild gloriously the bare feet
That run to bathe…
Du lieber Gott!

And after, ere the night is born,
Do hares come out about the corn?
Oh, is the water sweet and cool,
Gentle and brown, above the pool?
And laughs the immortal river still
Under the mill, under the mill?
Say, is there beauty yet to find?
And certainty? And Quiet kind?
Deep meadows yet, for to forget
The lies, and truths, and pain?…oh! yet
Stands the Church clock at ten to three?
And is there honey still for tea?

from

Good-Night to the Season

Winthrop Mackworth Praed

Good-night to the Season! 'tis over!
Gay dwellings no longer are gay;
The courtier, the gambler, the lover,
Are scatter'd like swallows away:
There's nobody left to invite one,
Except my good uncle and spouse;
My mistress is bathing in Brighton
My patron is sailing at Cowes:
For want of a better employment,
Till Ponto and Don can get out,
I'll cultivate rural enjoyment,
And angle immensely for trout…

Good-night to the Season! – the flowers
Of the grand horticultural fête,
When boudoirs were quitted for bowers,
And the fashion was not to be late;
When all who had money and leisure
Grew rural o'er ices and wines,
All pleasantly toiling for pleasure,
All hungrily pining for pines,
And making of beautiful speeches,
And marring of beautiful shows,
And feeding on delicate peaches,
And treading on delicate toes.

Good-night to the Season – another
Will come with its trifles and toys,
And hurry away, like its brother,
In sunshine, and odour, and noise.
Will it come with a rose or a briar?
Will it come with a blessing or curse?
Will its bonnets be lower or higher?
Will its morals be better or worse?
Will it find me grown thinner or fatter,
Or fonder of wrong or of right,
Or married, – or buried? – no matter,
Good-night to the Season, Good-night!

...Come Sons of summer, by whose toil,
We are the Lords of Wine and Oil:
By whose tough labours, and rough hands,
We rip up first, then reap our lands...

Autumn

Poor Old Horse

Folk Song

My clothing was once of the linsey woolsey fine,
My tail it grew at length, my coat did likewise shine;
But now I'm growing old; my beauty does decay,
My master frowns upon me; one day I heard him say,

Poor old horse: poor old horse.

Once I was kept in the stable snug and warm,
To keep my tender limbs from any cold or harm;
But now in open fields, I am forced for to go,
In all sorts of weather, let it be hail, rain, freeze or snow.

Poor old horse: poor old horse.

Once I was fed on the very best corn and hay
That ever grew in yon fields, or in yon meadows gay;
But now there's no such doing can I find at all,
I'm glad to pick the green sprouts that grow behind yon wall.

Poor old horse: poor old horse.

"You are old, you are cold, you are deaf, dull, dumb and slow,
You are not fit for anything, or in my team to draw.
You have eaten all my hay, you have spoiled all my straw,
So hang him, whip him, stick him, to the huntsman let him go."

Poor old horse: poor old horse.

My hide unto the tanners then I would freely give,
My body to the hound dogs, I would rather die than live,
Likewise my poor old bones that have carried you many a mile,
Over hedges, ditches, brooks, bridges, likewise gates and stiles.

Poor old horse: poor old horse.

The Solitary Reaper

William Wordsworth

Behold her, single in the field,
Yon solitary Highland Lass!
Reaping and singing by herself;
Stop here, or gently pass!
Alone she cuts and binds the grain,
And sings a melancholy strain;
Oh listen! for the Vale profound
Is overflowing with the sound.

No Nightingales did ever chaunt
More welcome notes to weary bands
Of travellers in some shady haunt,
Among Arabian sands:
A voice so thrilling ne'er was heard
In springtime from the Cuckoo-bird,
Breaking the silence of the seas
Among the farthest Hebrides.

Will no one tell me what she sings? –
Perhaps the plaintive numbers flow
For old, unhappy, far-off things,
And battles long ago:
Or is it some more humble lay,
Familiar matter of today?
Some natural sorrow, loss, or pain,
That has been, and may be again?

Whate'er the theme, the Maiden sang
As if her song could have no ending;
I saw her singing at her work,
And o'er the sickle bending; –
I listened motionless and still;
And, as I mounted up the hill,
The music in my heart I bore,
Long after it was heard no more.

Autumn

John Clare

The thistle down's flying, though the winds are all still,
On the green grass now lying, now mounting the hill,
The spring from the fountain now boils like a pot;
Through stones past the counting, it bubbles red-hot.

The ground parched and cracked is like overbaked bread,
The greensward all wracked is bents dried up and dead.
The fallow fields glitter like water indeed,
And gossamers twitter, flung from weed unto weed.

Hill-tops like hot iron glitter bright in the sun,
And the rivers we're eyeing burn to gold as they run;
Burning hot is the ground, liquid gold is the air;
Whoever looks round sees Eternity there.

To Autumn

John Keats

Season of mists and mellow fruitfulness,
Close bosom-friend of the maturing sun;
Conspiring with him how to load and bless
With fruit the vines that round the thatch-eves run;
To bend with apples the moss'd cottage-trees,
And fill all fruit with ripeness to the core;
To swell the gourd, and plump the hazel shells
With a sweet kernel; to set budding more
And still more, later flowers for the bees,
Until they think warm days will never cease;
For Summer has o'er-brimm'd their clammy cells.

Who hath not seen Thee oft amid thy store?
Sometimes whoever seeks abroad may find
Thee sitting careless on a granary floor,
Thy hair soft-lifted by the winnowing wind;
Or on a half-reaped furrow sound asleep,
Drowsed with the fume of poppies, while thy hook
Spares the next swath and all its twinéd flowers;
And sometimes like a gleaner thou dost keep
Steady thy laden head across a brook;
Or by a cider-press, with patient look,
Thou watchest the last oozings, hours by hours.

Where are the songs of Spring? Aye, where are they?
Think not of them, – thou hast thy music too,
Whilst barréd clouds bloom the soft-dying day
And touch the stubble-plains with rosy hue:
Then in a wailful choir the small gnats mourn
Among the river-sallows, borne aloft
Or sinking as the light wind lives or dies;
And full-grown lambs bleat from hilly bourn;
Hedge-crickets sing, and now with treble soft
The redbreast whistles from a garden-croft,
And gathering swallows twitter in the skies.

from

November

Robert Bridges

The lonely season in lonely lands, when fled
Are half the birds, and mists lie low, and the sun
Is rarely seen, nor strayeth far from his bed;
The short days pass unwelcomed one by one.

Out by the ricks the mantled engine stands
Crestfallen, deserted, – for now all hands
Are told to the plough, – and ere it is dawn appear
The teams following and crossing far and near,
As hour by hour they broaden the brown bands
Of the striped fields; and behind them firk and prance
The heavy rooks, and daws grey-pated dance:
As awhile, surmounting a crest, in sharp outline
(A miniature of toil, a gem's design,)
They are pictured, horses and men, or now near by
Above the lane they shout lifting the share,
By the trim hedgerow bloom'd with purple air;
Where, under the thorns, dead leaves in huddle lie
Packed by the gales of Autumn, and in and out
The small wrens glide
With a happy note of cheer,
And yellow amorets flutter above and about,
Gay, familiar in fear.

The Passing Day

William Ernest Henley

A late lark twitters from the quiet skies;
And from the west,
Where the sun, his day's work ended,
Lingers as in content,
There falls on the old, grey city
An influence luminous and serene,
A shining peace.

The smoke ascends
In a rosy-and-golden haze. The spires
Shine, and are changed. In the valley
Shadows rise. The lark sings on. The sun,
Closing his benediction,
Sinks, and the darkening air
Thrills with a sense of the triumphing night –
Night, with her train of stars
And her great gift of sleep.

So be my passing!
My task accomplished and the long day done,
My wages taken, and in my heart
Some late lark singing,
Let me be gathered to the quiet west,
The sundown splendid and serene,
Death.

from
Ode to the West Wind
Percy Bysshe Shelley

O wild West Wind, thou breath of Autumn's being,
Thou, from whose unseen presence the leaves dead
Are driven, like ghosts from an enchanter fleeing,

Yellow, and black, and pale, and hectic red,
Pestilence-stricken multitudes: O thou,
Who chariotest to their dark wintry bed

The wingéd seeds, where they lie cold and low,
Each like a corpse within its grave, until
Thine azure sister of the Spring shall blow

Her clarion o'er the dreaming earth, and fill
(Driving sweet buds like flocks to feed in air)
With living hues and odours plain and hill:

Wild Spirit, which art moving everywhere;
Destroyer and preserver; hear, oh, hear!

...Now winter nights enlarge, The number of their hours;
And clouds their storms discharge, Upon the airy towers,
Let now the chimneys blaze, And cups o'erflow with wine,
Let well-tun'd words amaze, With harmony divine...

Winter

Winter's Song

from
'Love's Labour's Lost'
William Shakespeare

When Icicles hang by the wall,
And Dick the Shepherd blows his nail;
And Tom bears Logs into the hall,
And Milk comes frozen home in pail:
When blood is nipt, and ways be foul
Then nightly sings the staring Owl
Tu-whit to-woo!
A merry note,
While greasy Joan doth keel the pot.

When all aloud the wind doth blow,
And coughing drowns the Parson's saw:
And birds sit brooding in the snow,
And Marian's nose looks red and raw:
When roasted Crabs hiss in the bowl,
When nightly sings the staring Owl,
Tu-whit to-woo!
A merry note,
While greasy Joan doth keel the pot.

Winter Evening

from
'The Task'
William Cowper

Now stir the fire, and close the shutters fast,
Let fall the curtains, wheel the sofa round,
And, while the bubbling and loud-hissing urn
Throws up a steamy column, and the cups,
That cheer but not inebriate, wait on each,
So let us welcome peaceful evening in…

Oh Winter, ruler of th'inverted year,…
I love thee, all unlovely as thou seemst,
And dreaded as thou art. Thou hold'st the sun
A prisoner in the yet undawning east,
Shortening his journey between morn and noon,
And hurrying him, impatient of his stay,
Down to the rosy west; but kindly still
Compensating his loss with the added hours
Of social converse and instructive ease,
And gathering, at short notice, in one group
The family dispersed, and fixing thought,
Not less dispersed by day-light and its cares.
I crown thee king of intimate delights,
Fire-side enjoyments, home-born happiness,
And all the comforts that the lowly roof
Of undisturbed retirement and the hours
Of long uninterrupted evening know.

On Ice

from

'The Prelude' Vol. 1

William Wordsworth

...All shod with steel
We hissed along the polished ice in games...
And not a voice was idle: with the din
Smitten, the precipices rang aloud;
The leafless trees and every icy crag
Tinkled like iron; while far distant hills
Into the tumult sent an alien sound
Of melancholy not unnoticed, while the stars
Eastward were sparkling clear, and in the west
The orange sky of evening died away.
Not seldom from the uproar I retired
Into a silent bay, or sportively
Glanced sideway, leaving the tumultuous throng,
To cut across the reflex of a star
That fled, and, flying still before me, gleamed
Upon the glassy plain: and oftentimes,
When we had given our bodies to the wind,
And all the shadowy banks on either side
Came sweeping through the darkness, spinning still
The rapid line of motion, then at once
Have I, reclining back upon my heels,
Stopped short; yet still the solitary cliffs
Wheeled by me – even as if the earth had rolled
With visible motion her diurnal round!
Behind me they did stretch in solemn train,
Feebler and feebler, and I stood and watched
Till all was tranquil as a dreamless sleep.

from

December 13, 1836

Emily Jane Brontë

High waving heather, 'neath stormy blasts bending,
Midnight and moonlight and bright shining stars;
Darkness and glory rejoicingly blending,
Earth rising to heaven and heaven descending,
Man's spirit away from its drear dongeon sending,
Bursting the fetters and breaking the bars.

All down the mountain sides, wild forests lending
One mighty voice to the life-giving wind;
Rivers their banks in the jubilee rending,
Fast through the valleys a reckless course wending,
Wilder and deeper their waters extending,
Leaving a desolate desert behind.

Shining and lowering and swelling and dying,
Changing for ever from midnight to noon;
Roaring like thunder, like soft music sighing,
Shadows on shadows advancing and flying,
Lightning-bright flashes and deep gloom defying,
Coming as swiftly and fading as soon.

The Darkling Thrush

Thomas Hardy

I leant upon a coppice gate
When Frost was spectre-gray,
And Winter's dregs made desolate
The weakening eye of day.
The tangled bine-stems scored the sky
Like strings of broken lyres,
And all mankind that haunted nigh
Had sought their household fires.

The land's sharp features seemed to be
The Century's corpse outleant,
His crypt the cloudy canopy,
The wind his death-lament.
The ancient pulse of germ and birth
Was shrunken hard and dry,
And every spirit upon earth
Seemed fervourless as I.

At once a voice arose among
The bleak twigs overhead
In a full-hearted evensong
Of joy illimited;
An aged thrush, frail, gaunt and small,
In blast-beruffled plume,
Had chosen thus to fling his soul
Upon the growing gloom.

So little cause for carolings
Of such ecstatic sound
Was written on terrestial things
Afar or nigh around,
That I could think there trembled through
His happy good-night air
Some blessed Hope, whereof he knew
And I was unaware.

Winter Nightfall

Robert Bridges

The day begins to droop, —
Its course is done:
But nothing tells the place
Of the setting sun.

The hazy darkness deepens,
And up the lane
You may hear, but cannot see,
The homing wain.

The engine pants and hums
In the farm hard by:
Its lowering smoke is lost
In the lowering sky.

The soaking branches drip
And all night through
The dropping will not cease
In the avenue.

A tall man there in the house
Must keep his chair:
He knows he will never again
Breathe the spring air:

His heart is worn with work;
He is giddy and sick
If he rise to go as far
As the nearest rick:

He thinks of his morn of life,
His hale, strong years;
And braves as he may the night
Of darkness and tears.

The Falconer and his Hawk

Anon

The soaring hawk from fist that flies,
Her Falconer doth constrain
Sometime to range the ground unknown
To find her out again:
And if by sight or sound of bell,
His falcon he may see,
Wo ho ho, he cries with cheerful voice,
The gladdest man is he.

By lure then in finest sort,
He seeks to bring her in,
But if she full gorgéd be,
He can not so her win:
Although her becks and bending eyes,
She many proffers makes,
Wo ho ho, he cries, away she flies,
And so her leave she takes.

This woeful man with weary limbs
Runs wand'ring round about:
At length by noise of chattering pies,
His hawk again found out,
His heart was glad his eyes had seen
His falcon swift of flight:
Wo ho ho, he cries, she empty gorged,
Upon his lure doth light.

How glad was then the falconer there,
No pen nor tongue can tell:
He swam in bliss that lately felt
Like pains of cruel hell.
His hand sometime upon her train,
Sometime upon her breast
Wo ho ho, he cries with cheerful voice,
His heart was now at rest.

My dear, likewise behold thy love,
What pains he doth endure:
And now at length let pity move
To stoop unto his lure
A hood of silk and silver bells,
New gifts I promise thee:
Wo ho ho, I cry, I come then say,
Make me as glad as he.

from

In Memorium

Alfred, Lord Tennyson

To-night the winds begin to rise
And roar from yonder dropping day:
The last red leaf is whirl'd away,
And rooks are blown about the skies;

The forest crack'd, the water curl'd,
The cattle huddled on the lea;
And wildly dash'd on tower and tree
The sunbeam strikes along the world:

And but for fancies, which aver
That all thy motions gently pass
Athwart a plane of molten glass,
I scarce could brook the strain and stir

That makes the barren branches loud;
And but for fear it is not so,
The wild unrest that lives in woe
Would dote and pore on yonder cloud

That rises upward always higher,
And onward drags a labouring breast,
And topples round the dreary west,
A looming bastion fringed with fire.

The Snowdrop

Anna Laetitia Barbauld

Already now the snowdrop dares appear,
The first pale blossom of th' unripen'd year;
As Flora's breath, by some transforming power,
Had chang'd an icicle into a flower,
Its name and hue the scentless plant retains,
And winter lingers in its icy veins.

Index of first lines

NB: First lines of extracts are denoted by brackets. Where helpful, the first line of the complete poem is the line above.

Picture list

6 *Harvest*, from *Summer* (detail) by Francisco de Lucientes Goya; 8 & 9 *The Awakening of Adonis* by John William Waterhouse; 11 *Trees and Crows*, from *Winter*, called *Snow* (detail) by Charles Daubigny; 12 *Lambs symbolising apostles* – mosaic in sixth-century choir. Location: San Apollinare in Classe Ravenna; 15 *A Shepherd Piper* by Pieter Wtewael; 16 *Washerwomen* by Camille Pissarro; 18 *The Shepherdess* by Francesco Paulo; 20 *Dancing Maidens* by Leopold Franz Kowalsky; 22 *The Haymaker* by George Clausen; 24 *Blackbird* by Comte G. L. L. De Buffon; 27 *Landscape with Shepherd and Peasants* by Jacob van Ruisdael; 28 *La Primavera* (Spring) detail by Fillipepi Sandro Botticelli; 30 *Flowers in a Meadow* by Guiseppe Pellizza da Volpedo; 32 & 33 *The Garden 1870* by Demetrio Cosola; 34 Illustration of Midsummer Night's Dream by Warwick Goble; 36 *Autumn* by Guiseppe Arcimboldo; 38 *Dutch Kitchen Maid* by Hermann Knopf; 41 *Mullino Canal, England* by John Constable; 42 *Moonlight Sonata* by Ralph Albert Blakelock; 44 Illustration in Scribners Magazine, April 1910 – PreRaphelite female by Charles A. Winter; 47 *Two Horses* by Albert Beirstadt; 48 Illustration in *The Studio*, 1902, *Ladies in Garden* by William Rankin; 51 Illustration of 'the Story of the Fisherman' by Edmund Dulac; 52 Illustration – *The Ecstatic Boy* by Margaret C. Cook; 54 *In the Bayou* by Joseph Rusling Meeker; 56 *Resting under the Lilacs* or *Lilacs in Grey Weather* by Claude Monet; 58 *Man Fishing in New England Stream* by Winslow Homer; 60 & 61 *Les Quatre Heures de la Journée les Vespres (The Four Stages of the Day: Vespers)* by Louis Joseph Watteau; 63 *Girl and Horse*, nineteenth century. Source: E. K. Johnson in 'Sunbeams'; 64 *Reaper Woman* by Grigori Grigorievich Miassoledov; 66 *Landscape 1895* by Isidro Nonell; 69 *Landscape at Gers* by Charles de, Comte d'Artangnan Montesquiou; 71 *The Return of the Herd (La Reutrée du Troupeau)* by Constant Troyon; 72 *Hill with Ploughed Field* by Caspar David Friedrich; 75 *Windswept Landscape* by Camille Corot; 76 & 77 *Moonlight, Skating in Central Park* by John O'Brien Inman; 78 *Hunters in the Snow* by Pieter Brueghel the Elder; 81 *Family by the Fire 1869*, Illustration in Gray's 'Elegy'; 83 *Winter Landscape with Ice Skaters* by Jan van de Cappleel; 85 *Lake Buttermere* by Joseph Mallord William Turner; 86 *La Pie 1869-9* by Claude Monet; 88 *Deer near house* by C. F. Aagaard in 'Illustreret Tidende'; 91 *Falcons*, eighteenth-century French watercolour by unknown artist; 92 *Walk at Dusk* by Caspar David Friedrich; 95 *The Snowdrop & Crocus Galanthus* from 'The Temple of Flora' by R. J. Thornton